Cambridge
Primary
Reading
Anthologies

1

Student's Book
with Online Audio

CAMBRIDGE
UNIVERSITY PRESS

Scope and Sequence

Unit 1 What is a family?

	Genre	Key Words	Reading Strategy
Fiction *Where's that Smile?*	Poetry	smile, share, hair, twins, stop, fun	Identifying Setting
Nonfiction *A Very Special Person in My Life*	Personal Profile	beard, together, hug (n), pick, yummy, food	Predicting from Pictures

Unit 2 What is school like?

	Genre	Key Words	Reading Strategy
Fiction *A Class for Kitties*	Fantasy	playground, run, bounce, climb, rope, helpful	Predicting from Titles
Nonfiction *Snacks for After School*	Recipe	hungry, healthy, wash, cut, peel, sprinkle	Understanding the Meaning of Words in Context

Unit 3 What are living things?

	Genre	Key Words	Reading Strategy
Fiction *Ally and the Ants*	Realistic Fiction	sticky, sweet, paw, lick, hurt, wet	Cause and Effect
Nonfiction *The Amazing World of Ants*	Nature Blog	tunnel, bridge, dirt, carry, protect, bite	Understanding Sequence

Unit 4 What is a friend?

	Genre	Key Words	Reading Strategy
Fiction *The Selfish Giant*	Fairy Tale	garden, shout, scared, spring, selfish, lonely	Identifying Setting
Nonfiction *Best Friends Forever*	Email	miss (v), new, parrot, noisy, cute, pet (v)	Identifying the Main Idea

Unit 5 How do we have fun?

	Genre	Key Words	Reading Strategy
Fiction *My Best Friend, Oliver the Chameleon*	Fantasy	change, hide, alone, magical, strawberry, noise	Identifying Characters
Nonfiction *Make Your Own Toys*	Instructional Text on Crafts	straw, hole, fold, kick, rubber band, shoot	Identifying the Main Idea

Unit 6 How can we help?

Fiction *Oh, Butterfingers!*	Realistic Fiction	drop, goalie, butter, salt, cake, careful	Identifying Key Details
Nonfiction *Mom's List*	Instructions/List	feed, drink (v), water (v), dinner, early, late	Identifying the Main Idea

Unit 7 Why do we need plants and animals?

Fiction *The Giant Turnip*	Russian Folktale	farm, plant (v), fall, harvest, giant, delicious	Visualizing
Nonfiction *Amazing Plants*	Magazine Article on Biology	smell (v), poisonous, branch, leaf, insect, weigh	Using Captions

Unit 8 What is imagination?

Fiction *Imagine That!*	Realistic Fiction	kiss (v), sleepy, carpet, secret, boat, huge	Summarizing
Nonfiction *A Sea Creature of Your Imagination*	Instructional Text on Arts and Crafts	amazing, creature, strange, wave, stripes, spots	Understanding Sequence

Unit 9 Why do we need clothes?

Fiction *My Hat Is Dancing on My Head*	Poetry	hat, head, shirt, back, hang, rack	Identifying Main Idea and Details
Nonfiction *Happy Feet Around the World*	Cultural Studies Magazine Article	sandals, protect, step on, leather, strong, fur	Making Text-to-Self Connections

What is a family?

Key Words

1 🎧 **Preview the Key Words.**

smile   share   hair

twins   stop   fun

2 **Circle the two Key Words that show you are happy.**

t w i n s f u n s t o p s h a r e s m i l e h a i r

3 **Which word means *sisters* or *brothers*? Circle.**

fun   twins   share

Pre-reading

4 📖 **Look at the pictures on pages 5–9. Read and circle.**

Where are the children?

a   at school   b   at home   c   at the toy store

5 🎧 **Listen and read.**

Where's That Smile?

By Jeremy Edgar

Illustrated by Luis Montiel

Happy birthday, Kyle!
Where's that smile?
It's time to play
on your special day.
Come on, Kyle!
Where's that smile?
Why are you sad?
Why are you mad?

Why am I sad?
Why am I mad?
I have to share
with my sister Claire
and her awesome hair!
You see, we're two,
and it's her day, too!
We're twins, you see.
It's not just me.
I have to share
with my sister Claire
and her awesome hair!

When the girls and boys
come with presents and toys,
we start to play
on our special day.
Then, here comes Claire
with her awesome hair.
They stop and stare
at her amazing hair.
It isn't fair.
They don't see me there!

Don't be sad,
and don't be mad.
You and me,
we're alike, you see!
All the fun and joy
are inside you, boy!
Just let them out
And play and shout.
Now it's time to play
on your special day.
Come on, Kyle!
Where's that smile?

Here come the girls and boys
with their presents and toys.
"Look!" they say, "Here comes Claire
with her awesome hair!
And here comes Kyle
with his birthday smile!
Now let's play
on their special day."

They play and they run
and have lots of fun.
And now it's time
for Dad to climb
and hang the donkey
from the garden tree.
With a big smile,
it says to Kyle,
"All the fun and joy,
are inside me, Boy."

At the end of the day,
the kids all say
goodbye to Claire
with her awesome hair
and goodbye to Kyle
with his amazing smile.
Today he learns something new.
What the piñata says is really true:
All the fun and joy are inside of YOU!

Key Words

1 Find the Key Words in the word search.

A	Z	Q	H	E	F	L
S	S	S	A	R	E	J
M	B	T	I	A	K	G
I	P	O	R	H	T	M
L	R	P	N	S	W	O
E	S	M	L	I	I	T
A	T	R	P	F	N	N
F	U	N	D	D	S	V

2 Circle the correct Key Word.

a I stop / share my crayons.

b Claire has awesome hair / smile.

c The children stop / share and stare at Claire.

d The party is smile / fun.

e Kyle has an amazing hair / smile.

Comprehension

3 Circle *Kyle* or *Claire*.

a Who is sad?   Kyle   Claire

b Who has awesome hair?   Kyle   Claire

c Who is Kyle's twin?   Claire   Dad

d Who has an amazing smile?   Kyle   Claire

e Who hangs the piñata from the tree? Claire   Dad

f Who learns something new?   Kyle   Claire

4 Number the sentences in order.

a Dad hangs the piñata.   _____

b Kyle is sad.   _1_

c Kyle learns something new.   _____

d The boys and girls say goodbye.   _____

e The boys and girls play.   _____

Digging Deeper

5 **Why is Kyle sad? Circle the correct option.**

   a Because his sister Claire has awesome hair.

   b Because the piñata is sad.

   c Because he has to share his birthday with his twin.

6 **Read the poem again. Match words that rhyme.**

   a sad   fun

   b Claire   boys

   c play   smile

   d Kyle   day

   e toys   hair

   f run   mad

7 **What makes Kyle and Claire twins? Mark (✔) three options.**

   a They have the same mom and dad. ☐

   b They share a birthday. ☐

   c They both like cake. ☐

   d They are the same age. ☐

Personalization

8 **Draw yourself with awesome hair and an amazing smile.**

9 **What animal or superhero is your birthday piñata? Draw and color.**

1 What is a family?

Key Words

1 🎧 **Preview the Key Words.**
1.3

beard   together   hug (n)

pick   yummy   food

2 **Complete the sentences with the Key Words.**

a My favorite ___ o ___ d is pasta.

b Dad's ___ e ___ ___ d is brown.

c We ___ i ___ k apples from the tree.

d Give your friend a ___ u ___. It's his birthday!

e Pete and Mark go to school ___ o ___ ___ t ___ e ___ .

f Chocolate cake is ___ ___ m ___ y!

Pre-reading

3 📖 **Look at the photos on pages 13–15. Match.**

a They are grandmother and granddaughter.

b They are mother and daughter.

c They are father and son.

4 🎧 **Listen and read.**
1.4

A Very Special Person in My Life

Name: Yusuf
Age: 5 years old
Country: Turkey
Special Person: My father

My name is Yusuf.
I live in Turkey. I'm five years old.

This is my father. He has
brown hair and a beard.
My father is very special to me.

We play together. I ride my bike.
My father helps me!

We play until sunset.
Then, we walk home.
We hold hands.

Name: Ana
Age: 6 years old
Country: Italy
Special Person: Nonna

My name is Ana. I live in Italy. I'm six years old.

This is my grandmother. I call her Nonna. She is special to me. She gives me big hugs.

Nonna has a garden. She grows tomatoes. I pick them for lunch. It's fun!

My brother also helps Nonna cook.

Nonna makes pasta. It's yummy! It's my favorite food.

Name: María
Age: 8 years old
Country: Argentina
Special Person: My mother

My name is María.
I'm eight years old.
I live in Argentina.

This is my mother.
She has brown eyes and
long hair. Like me!
My mother is my best friend.
We have fun together!

We play hand
games together.

We read stories on my tablet.
My father and brother also play with us.
I love my family.

Key Words

1 Label the pictures with the Key Words.

a h__ __   b p__ __ __   c b__ __ __ __   d y__ __ __ __

Comprehension

2 Who is special to them? Write *mother*, *father*, or *grandmother*.

a _____   b _____   c _____

3 Write *Y* for Yusuf, *A* for Ana, or *M* for María.

a Italy ☐

b pasta ☐

c bike ☐

d tablet ☐

e Turkey ☐

f Argentina ☐

4 Circle *Yes* or *No*.

a Ana is seven years old.   Yes   No

b Yusuf and his father play together.   Yes   No

c Yusuf lives in Mexico.   Yes   No

d María has short hair.   Yes   No

e Nonna has a garden.   Yes   No

f Ana's mother is her best friend.   Yes   No

Digging Deeper

5 **Underline the correct option.**

1 Why is Yusuf's father special to him?

    a because his father plays with him

    b because his father has brown hair

2 Why do Yusuf and his father hold hands?

    a because they're mad

    b because they're happy together

3 Why is Nonna special to Ana?

    a because Nonna cooks with her brother

    b because Nonna gives her big hugs

4 Why is pasta Ana's favorite food?

    a because it's yummy

    b because it has tomatoes

5 How are María and her mother alike?

    a they both have brown eyes and long hair

    b they both have black eyes and long hair

6 Why do María and her mother have fun?

    a because they play hand games together

    b because they live in Argentina

Personalization

6 **Draw a special person in your life.**

7 **Complete these sentences about the special person in your life.**

My _____ is very special.

His / Her name is _____.

He / She lives in _____.

2 What is school like?

Key Words

1 🎧 **Preview the Key Words.**
2.1

playground

run

bounce

climb

rope

helpful

2 Write the three Key Words that are actions.

_____ _____ _____

Pre-reading

3 📖 **Look at the pictures on pages 19–21. Then, circle the correct options.**

1 Where are the animals?

   a at home   b at a zoo   c in school

2 What kind of animals are the students?

   a dogs   b cats   c birds

3 What animal is the teacher?

   a mouse   b cat   c dog

4 🎧 **Listen and read.**
2.2

A Class for Kitties

By Sarah Steinberg
Illustrated by Laura González

This is the playground.
It's time to go to class, kitties.
Line up, please! Don't be late.
It's time for reading. It's time for writing.
It's time for math.
Are these little kittens ready for school?
Yes, they are ready!
Can you see the teacher? There she is!
Good morning, Ms. Romero.
Good morning, little kitties.

This is the classroom. These are the desks.
All the kitties sit nicely at their desks.
Good morning Moe, and Eunice, and Steven, and Raf.

"Good morning, class," says Ms. Romero.
"Please take out your books."

The students take out their books.
Oh no! Eunice forgot her books today.
She is sad. She hides her face behind her paws.

Moe has an idea. He raises his hand.
"Ms. Romero, can I share my book with Eunice?"
What a good idea! That is very kind, Moe.

It is time for P.E. class.
The kitties love P.E.!
In the gym, they run, bounce balls,
and climb ropes.
The kittens go to the gym in a line.
The gym door is closed.
Raf holds the door open for his
teacher and classmates.
That is very helpful, Raf! Thank you.

At snack time, the kitties have milk to drink.
Please kitties, don't crowd. Wait your turn.

It is time to go home.
The kitties are ready.
They are ready to see their families.
But where is Steven?

"Where are you, Steven?" asks Ms. Romero.
Look, there he is! He's on the window ledge.

"Steven, be careful!" shouts Ms. Romero.
How does Steven get down?
He's a kitten! He can jump!

Key Words

1 **Complete the Key Words.**

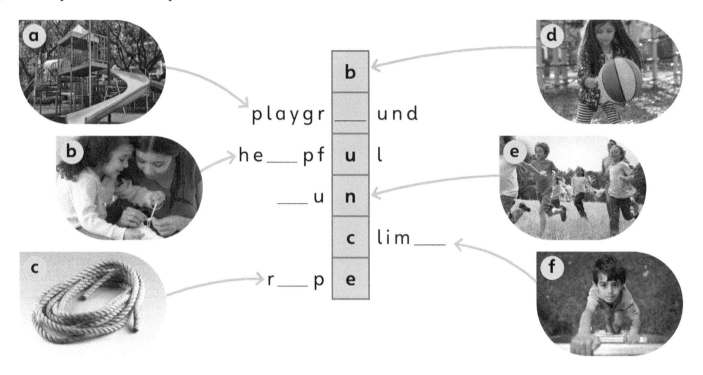

playgr ___ und

he ___ pf **u** l

___ u **n**

c lim ___

r ___ p **e**

b
u
n
c
e

Comprehension

2 **Match the questions to the correct kitty.**

a Who is sad?

b Who is helpful?

c Who climbs on the window ledge?

Raf

Steven

Eunice

3 **Where do the kitties do the activities? Match.**

1 climb ropes   2 line up   3 take out their books

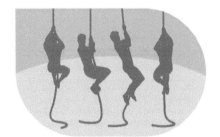  

a playground   b classroom   c gym

Digging Deeper

4 **Match the problem to the solution.**

Problem	Solution
I Steven is on the window ledge.	a Raf holds the door open.
2 Eunice forgets her book.	b Moe shares his book with Eunice.
3 The gym door is closed.	c He's a kitten! He can jump!

5 **What happens next? Draw Steven jumping from the window ledge.**

Personalization

6 **Circle your favorite activity.**

playing at the park   playing soccer   hiking   riding a bike

7 **Draw yourself doing the activity.**

(2) What is school like?

Key Words

1 🎧 **Preview the Key Words.**
2.3

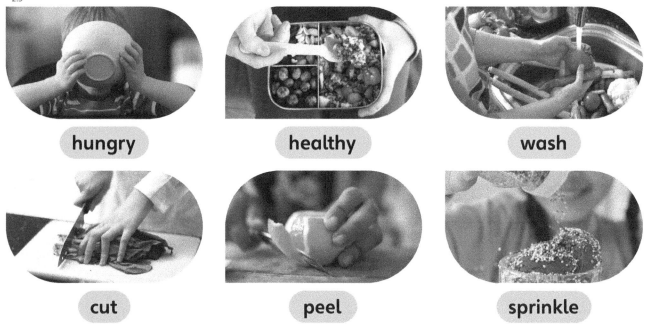

hungry

healthy

wash

cut

peel

sprinkle

2 **Circle the correct Key Word.**

a Tomatoes are a healthy / hungry food.

b I want some ice cream. I'm healthy / hungry!

c First, peel / sprinkle the banana. Then, you can eat it!

Pre-reading

3 **Look at the titles and pictures on pages 25–27. Match each title with the correct snack.**

Banana Pops   Rainbow Fruit Sticks   Ants on a Log

4 🎧 **Listen and read.**
2.4

SNACKS

for After School

By Maggie Pane

Are you hungry after school?
Look at these yummy snacks.
They're easy to make. And they're healthy to eat!

Ants on a Log

Ingredients

2 celery sticks   cream cheese   raisins or black olives

1 Wash the celery.

2 Cut the celery.
  (Ask an adult to help!)

3 Spread cream cheese
  inside each celery stick.

4 Put raisins or black
  olives on top.

Banana Pops

Bananas are healthy and delicious!

Ingredients

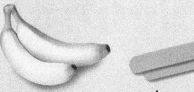

2 bananas

wooden sticks

yogurt

chopped nuts

chocolate sprinkles

1 Peel the bananas.

2 Put the bananas on wooden sticks.

3 Dip your banana pops into the yogurt.

4 Sprinkle chopped nuts or chocolate sprinkles on your banana pops.

Rainbow Fruit Sticks

Make colorful fruit sticks. Yum!

Ingredients

your favorite fruits of different colors (strawberries, grapes, cantaloupe, pineapple, kiwi)

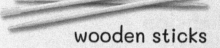

wooden sticks

yogurt

1 Wash and peel the fruit.

2 Cut the fruit. (Ask an adult to help!)

3 Put the fruit on wooden sticks.

4 Dip your fruit sticks into the yogurt.

Key Words

1 Look at the pictures. Label them *cut*, *sprinkle*, or *wash*.

a _____ b _____ c _____

Comprehension

2 What are the snacks similar to? Match.

Ants on a Log

Banana Pops

Rainbow Fruit Sticks

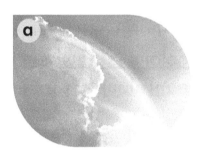
a

b

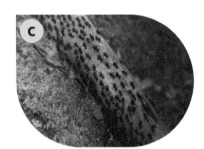
c

3 Number the steps for making Banana Pops in order.

____ Sprinkle chopped nuts or chocolate sprinkles on your banana pops.

____ Dip your banana pops into the yogurt.

__1__ Peel the bananas.

____ Put the bananas on wooden sticks.

__5__ Eat your banana pop!

Digging Deeper

4 📖 **You need *yogurt* and *sticks* for two snacks. Circle them in** green.

   a Banana Pops   b Rainbow Fruit Sticks   c Ants on a Log

5 📖 **You don't *peel* in this recipe. Circle the snack in** red.

   a Banana Pops   b Rainbow Fruit Sticks   c Ants on a Log

Personalization

6 **Which of the snacks above is your favorite? Why?**

My favorite snack is _____ because _____

_____.

7 **Change one ingredient in one of the snacks. Draw the new snack.**

8 **What is your new snack called?**

_____

3 What are living things?

Key Words

1 **Preview the Key Words.**
3.1

sticky

sweet

paw

lick

hurt

wet

2 **Write the Key Words related to the pictures.**

a _____

b _____

c _____

Pre-reading

3 **Look at the pictures on pages 31–37. Mark (✔) the correct option.**

1   What's the problem?

   a   There are ants in the garden. ☐

   b   There are ants in the kitchen. ☐

2   Who solves the problem?

   a   The girl and her dad. ☐

   b   The girl and her mom. ☐

4 **Listen and read.**
3.2

Ally and the Ants

By Joep van der Werff

Illustrated by Claudia Navarro

Ally walks into the kitchen. Her cat, Tom, sits on the floor.
Tom is playing with something. What is Tom doing?
Ally looks closely. He is playing with some ants!
Lots of ants!

"Why are there ants in the kitchen?" Ally asks.

"Meow!" answers Tom.

"Food? Yes, Tom," says Ally.
"There's something sticky on
the floor. It's ice cream. The
ants like sweet food. They're
walking in a line. Look!
They're eating the ice cream!"

Ice Cream

Ally says, "Ants, you can't stay here in the kitchen! Go back to the garden!"

But the ants don't listen. How can she get the ants to go back outside?

"Meow!" says Tom.

"Yes, of course!" says Ally. "Ants like sweet food. And jam is sweet. Let's put a line of jam on the floor. A line from the kitchen to the garden ... Look, Tom! They like it!"

But soon there are more and more ants!
Ally is worried. Where do they all come from?

"Dad doesn't want ants in the kitchen, Tom.
We have to get them out of here!"

Ally looks at her cat.

"Oh, no! Poor Tom!" she says.
"The ants are on your paws!"

Tom licks the ants off his paws.

"What can we do now?" asks Ally.

"Meow!" says Tom.

"With water? Good idea!" says Ally. "We can use water to move the ants back to the garden."

Ally puts her stool next to the sink. Now she can turn on the water!

She fills many cups with water. She pours the water on the floor around the ants.

But what happens? The ants swim happily in the water and jam. They love a sweet jam bath!

"Meow," Tom says. "Meow!"

"Yes, Tom. We need a squeegee to move the water outside," says Ally.

Ally gets a squeegee. She pulls the water toward the door.

Ally pulls gently. She doesn't want to hurt the ants! Finally, she moves all the water—with the ants—outside to the garden!

Ally's dad enters the kitchen.

"Hey, Ally, the floor looks a little wet," Dad says.

"There were ants, lots of them! I used water and the squeegee to move them into the garden," says Ally.

"Good job! I'm proud of you," says Dad.

"But the ants can still come back inside, Dad. Ants love jam and ice cream. Is there anything that they don't like?"

"Yes, there is!" Dad answers. "Ants don't like vinegar."

"Let's clean the kitchen floor with vinegar and water then," says Ally.

After a few minutes, the kitchen smells like vinegar.

Dad says, "No more ants in the house. Good work!"

Tom says, "Meow!"

And we understand what that means.
He says, "Great job, Ally!"

Key Words

1 **Unscramble the Key Words.**

a Ants like e – t – s – w – e _____ food.

b Cats lick their a – s – p – w _____.

c There is water on the floor. It's e – w – t _____.

d Ouch! My finger s – t – u – h – r _____.

e Do you i – k - l – c _____ your ice cream cone?

Comprehension

2 **Number the sentences in order.**

a The ants swim in the water and jam. ☐

b Ally walks into the kitchen and finds ants. 1

c Ally and her dad clean the floor with vinegar. ☐

d Ally puts a line of jam on the floor. ☐

e Ally pours water on the floor. ☐

f Ally uses a squeegee to move the ants outside. 5

3 **Match the causes to the effects.**

1 Ally puts jam on the floor.

2 Ally pours water on the floor.

3 Ally moves the ants to the garden with a squeegee.

a The ants enjoy a sweet jam bath.

b Her dad is happy.

c There are more ants in the kitchen.

4 **What do ants like? Mark (✔). What don't they like? Mark (✗).**

a ☐

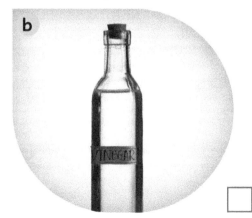

b ☐

Digging Deeper

5 Circle two things Tom refers to when he says "Meow!"

Personalization

6 Draw another food that ants like.

7 Draw your pet or your favorite animal. Draw a food it likes. Then, draw a food it doesn't like.

3 What are living things?

Key Words

1 🎧 **Preview the Key Words.**
3.3

tunnel

bridge

dirt

carry

protect

bite

2 **Complete the questions with Key Words. Then, answer the questions.**

a What do you usually _____ in your backpack?

_____

b What do you use to _____ yourself from the rain?

_____

c Do some ants _____? _____

Pre-reading

3 **Look at the pictures on pages 41–43. Cross out (✗) what is *not* in the text.**

a boy   b girl   c butterfly   d bee   e candy   f flower

4 🎧 **Listen and read.**
3.4

The Amazing World of Ants

Hi everyone! I'm Kim.
I love nature, and this is my secret world.
It's the amazing world of ants.

Come with me!

Ants are insects. They are my favorite insects. Do you know how many legs an insect has? It has six legs!

Ants live in colonies. A colony is a big group of ants.

You can find ants everywhere: on trees, in the grass, or underground.

Look at this colony!
There are lots of ants.

Ants are very good builders. They make tunnels and bridges with their bodies!

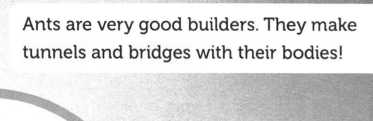

Where can we find ants? We can look for anthills. Anthills are piles of dirt or sand.

Ants make anthills when they build their tunnels.

Do you know what they eat? They eat seeds, vegetables, flowers, other insects, and even meat! Ants also love sugar. So don't leave sweet foods out!

When ants find food, they carry it to the anthill. Ants are really strong. They can carry things that weigh as much as 20 ants!

There is a queen in each colony. The queen is very important. She is the biggest ant in the colony. She has wings, and she lays eggs to make baby ants. Lots of eggs!

Look! Here are some worker ants. They protect the queen's eggs!

Be careful! Some ants can bite you when you touch them. But, most ants are friendly. I love ants!

Now you know a lot about ants. What's your favorite insect?

Key Words

1 Complete the Key Words and discover the hidden word. Then, match the words with the pictures.

a br ☐ dge
b tu ☐ nel
   s
c bit ☐
d ☐ arry
e dir ☐

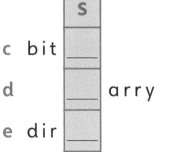

Comprehension

2 Write *Yes* or *No*.

a Ants are insects. _____
b Ants have eight legs. _____
c Ants live in anthills. _____
d Ants protect flowers. _____

3 Complete the sentences with words from the box.

queen	sugar	anthill	bridges

a Ants like _____.
b An _____ is a pile of dirt and sand.
c The biggest ant in the colony is the _____.
d Ants make tunnels and _____.

Digging Deeper

4 **Mark (✔) the correct option.**

Why is the queen important?

a She has wings. ☐

b She lays eggs. ☐

c She is big. ☐

5 🐜 **Number the facts in the order Kim talks about them.**

____ Ants carry food to their anthill.

____ Their queen lays eggs.

____ Ants make their anthill.

Personalization

6 **Draw an ant carrying something very big.**

7 **Draw your favorite insect. Then, write its name.**

This is a/an _____.

4 What is a friend?

Key Words

1 🎧 **Preview the Key Words.**
4.1

garden   shout   scared

spring   selfish   lonely

2 **Circle the correct Key Word.**

a There's a big tree in my spring / garden.

b She doesn't have any friends. She is scared / lonely.

c She shares her toys with her friends. She is not selfish / scared.

d There are lots of baby animals in spring / garden.

e I don't like bees. I'm selfish / scared of them.

f We are in a library. Don't shout / scared!

Pre-reading

3 📖 **Look at pages 47–51. Circle the setting.**

a children   b giant   c garden   d boy

4 🎧 **Listen and read.**
4.2

The Selfish Giant

By Oscar Wilde • Adapted by Lily Pane

Illustrated by Ismael Vázquez

The giant's garden is big and beautiful.

Can you hear that music? The birds are singing.

Can you smell the flowers? There are many flowers in the giant's garden.

Some children walk by the giant's castle. They see the giant's garden. They want to play there!

The giant is not home. The children start to play in the garden. It's fun! They play there all day.

Every day the children come to the garden and play. They are happy.

One day, the giant returns to his castle.
The children are playing in his garden.

The giant is angry. He shouts at the children.

"Go away! This is MY garden.
You cannot play here!"

The children are scared.
They run away.

"My garden is MY garden!"
says the giant.

The giant builds a very tall wall.
He makes a sign that says:

"THIS IS MY GARDEN. DO NOT ENTER."

The children are sad. The giant's garden is
their favorite place to play.

Spring comes, but it doesn't come to the giant's garden. The birds don't sing. The flowers don't bloom. The children don't come. They are scared. They are scared of the giant.

Summer asks, "Where are the children?" But no children come.

It's autumn now. There is fruit in many gardens. But there is no fruit in the giant's garden.

Autumn says, "No fruit for the giant. He is selfish."

Winter comes. The giant's garden is cold and gray. Winter stays for many years. The giant is lonely in his cold, dark castle. He is sad.

49

One day, a bird wakes the giant up. It is singing.

The giant looks out the window. He is surprised. He sees a little hole in the wall.

There are children in his garden again! They are climbing the trees. There are flowers. There are birds. Spring is in the garden, too!

The giant sees a little boy. The boy wants to climb a tree, but he can't. He is too small.

The giant goes outside to the garden. The children and Spring see the giant. They run away! But the little boy is not scared. He stays.

The giant helps the little boy climb up the tree. The boy is happy. The giant is happy, too.

The children see the giant smiling. They are no longer scared. They return to the garden. Spring returns to the garden, too.

The giant takes an ax and breaks the wall.

"It's your garden now, children," says the giant.

Every day, the children play in the giant's garden. The giant plays there, too.

The garden is beautiful again. Spring is always there.

Key Words

1 Cross out (✗) the Key Word that is *not* related to the giant.

selfish   lonely   scared   shout

Comprehension

2 **How do the children feel? Circle.**

a	at the beginning of the story	happy	scared	angry
b	in the middle of the story	happy	scared	angry
c	at the end of the story	happy	scared	angry

3 **How does the giant feel? Circle.**

a	when he comes home	happy	lonely	angry
b	when it's winter in the garden	happy	lonely	angry
c	at the end of the story	happy	lonely	angry

4 **Mark (✔) two bad things the giant does.**

a He shouts at the children. ☐

b He builds a tall wall. ☐

c He helps the little boy. ☐

d He breaks the wall. ☐

5 🔖 **The giant is selfish. What happens? Circle two pictures.**

a

c

b

Digging Deeper

6 **Autumn says "No fruit for the giant." Why?**

 a   Because Autumn is scared of the giant.

 b   Because the giant is selfish.

 c   Because Autumn is selfish.

7 **At the end, Spring is always in the garden. Why?**

 a   Because the giant is lonely.

 b   Because Spring is selfish.

 c   Because the giant isn't selfish anymore.

Personalization

8 **Draw the giant's garden in winter and in spring.**

9 **Are you selfish? Draw objects that you share with friends and family.**

Key Words

1 🎧 **Preview the Key Words.**
4.3

miss (v)   new   parrot

noisy   cute   pet (v)

2 Circle the two words that relate to animals.

pet   miss   parrot

Pre-reading

3 **Look at the pictures on page 55 and answer the questions.**

a How many animals can you see? _____

b What are they? _____

c How many children can you see? _____

d Are they boys or girls? _____

4 🎧 **Listen and read.**
4.4

Best Friends Forever

bubblemail.com

To: Sue Anderson <suegirl@net.com>
From: Laura Rodriguez <laurod@net.com>
Subject: Miss you!

Hi Sue,

I miss you a lot! Do you like your new house? What's your new bedroom like?

How's your parrot, Fluffy? Is he still noisy?

I have a photo of you and me. I always look at it. You're my best friend forever!

Take care,
Laura

P.S. Here's a photo of my puppy. His name is Clyde!

bubblemail.com

To: Laura Rodriguez <laurod@net.com>
From: Sue Anderson <suegirl@net.com>
Subject: Miss you, too!

Hi Laura,

I miss you, too!
I love our new house. My new bedroom is yellow and pink. Fluffy is still noisy, and he always says your name! Here's a photo of him. He doesn't like our new house. He stays in his cage all the time.
Poor Fluffy!

Your puppy is so cute! I want to pet him!
You're my BFF, too!

Talk soon!

Sue

Key Words

① Match the Key Words to what they refer to in the emails.

noisy　　　cute　　　new

 a

 b

 c

Comprehension

② Circle *Yes* or *No*.

a	Laura and Sue have pets.	Yes	No
b	They miss each other.	Yes	No
c	Laura sends a photo of Fluffy.	Yes	No
d	Sue's new bedroom is pink and blue.	Yes	No
e	Fluffy likes the new house.	Yes	No

③ 📖 Underline the main idea of the emails.

a Laura and Sue have pets.

b Laura and Sue miss each other.

c Fluffy is noisy.

d The puppy is cute.

④ Replace the word in bold with the correct word.

a The parrot is still **cute**. _____

b The **puppy** always says Laura's name. _____

c The parrot's name is **Poncho**. _____

d **Laura** has a new house. _____

e The puppy is **noisy**. _____

Digging Deeper

5 What does "BFF" mean? Mark (✔) the correct option.

a Best Friend Forever ☐

b Best Fluffy Friend ☐

c Be Funny, Friend ☐

6 How do you think Fluffy feels in the new house? Circle.

a lonely   b scared   c happy

Personalization

7 Draw yourself with your best friend or favorite pet.

8 Write an email to your BFF or to a good friend.

New Message

To: _____

From: _____

Subject: _____

Hi _____ ,

_____

_____

Take care,

_____

5 How do we have fun?

Key Words

1 🎧 **Preview the Key Words.**
5.1

change   hide   alone

magical   strawberry   noise

2 **Circle the correct Key Word.**

a Where are my friends? I'm alone / magical.

b Where are you? Don't hide / change behind the sofa.

c The hen in the fairy tale is alone / magical. It lays golden eggs!

d That noise / strawberry is green. Don't eat it!

e What's that noise / alone? Is it an airplane?

f Your pajamas are dirty. Hide / Change them!

Pre-reading

3 📖 **Read the title and look at the pictures on pages 59–61. Circle the characters.**

Dad   chameleon   dog   girl   Mom   boy

4 🎧 **Listen and read.**
5.2

My Best Friend, Oliver the Chameleon

By Melissa Kitson
Illustrated by Mónica Cahue

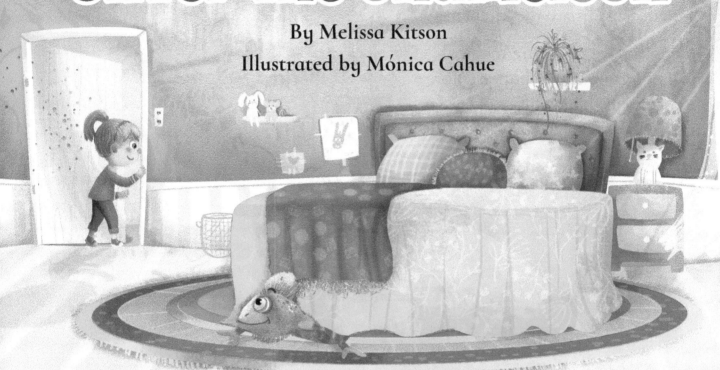

My name is Lucy, and I have a secret. My best friend is a chameleon!

This is Oliver. He lives in my bedroom. My mom and dad do not know about him. Oliver is very good at hiding. He can change color and stay very still.

But Oliver does not like to hide for long.

"Please Lucy, can we play now?" he asks.

I check first. We are alone!

"Yes, come out! Let's make a drawing."

We sit down with colored markers and paper. I draw a scary monster. It has big teeth and giant claws. Oliver draws a fluffy sheep.

"Now what do you want to do?" Oliver asks.

"Do you want to bake cookies?" I ask.

"Yes!" he answers. Oliver loves baking.
We go downstairs to the kitchen.

The cookies we make are magical.
They make your face change color.
My face turns blue. Oliver's face
turns red.

"You look like a strawberry!"
I laugh.

"Now what do you want to do?" Oliver asks.

"Let's play hide-and-seek!" I say.

Oliver smiles. He is very good at that game.
I count to ten, and Oliver hides.

"It's time to find you!" I say.

I look in the closet, but he is not there.
I look under the table, but he is not there.
I look behind the chair, but he is not there.

"Where are you Oliver?" I ask.

"Here I am!" says Oliver.

He is on top of the rug.

"What do you want to do now?" Oliver asks.

"Let's dance!" I say.

"Great! I love dancing," says Oliver.

I put on music, and we start to dance.
It is so much fun! Then, I hear the door open.

"Oh, no! It's Mom and Dad," I say.

Oliver hides behind the chair.

"Lucy! What is all that noise?" Mom asks.

"Nothing," I say.

She and Dad look around the room.

"Is someone else here?" Dad asks.

"No," I say. "It's just me."

Mom sighs. "Why don't you find a
friend to play with?" she asks.

"I have a friend," I say.
"But he is very hard to find!"

Key Words

1 **Match the sentence halves.**

a   A chameleon **changes**   **alone** in the bedroom.

b   Oliver's face   are **magical**.

c   The cookies   looks like a **strawberry**.

d   Oliver   color.

e   Lucy and Oliver are   a **noise**.

f   Mom hears   **hides** on the rug.

Comprehension

2 **How do Lucy and Oliver have fun? Mark (✔) the correct options.**

dance ☐   bake cookies ☐   write ☐

jump rope ☐   play hide-and-seek ☐   read stories ☐

draw ☐   sing songs ☐   watch TV ☐

3 **Write *Lucy* or *Oliver*.**

a   Who draws a monster?   _____

b   Who is hard to find?   _____

c   Who counts to ten?   _____

d   Who puts on the music?   _____

e   Who looks like a strawberry? _____

f   Who hides behind a chair?   _____

4 **Write *T* (true) or *F* (false).**

a   Oliver is a monster.   _____

b   Lucy and Oliver bake cookies.   _____

c   Lucy plays with her brother.   _____

d   Lucy's dad hears a noise.   _____

e   Lucy's best friend is Oliver.   _____

Digging Deeper

5 **How are the cookies magical? Circle.**

a The cookies are different colors.

b They make Lucy and Oliver's faces change colors.

c The cookies are yummy.

6 **Why does Oliver change color? Circle.**

a He's a secret friend.

b He's scared.

c He's a chameleon.

Personalization

7 **How do you have fun? Mark (✔) or write your favorite activities.**

play soccer ☐   dance ☐   bake cookies ☐   draw ☐

jump rope ☐   read stories ☐   ride your bike ☐   paint ☐

_____   _____   _____

8 **Draw your bedroom and hide a secret friend in it.**

9 **What do you and your secret friend do?**

_____

5 How do we have fun?

Key Words

1 🎧 Preview the Key Words.
5.3

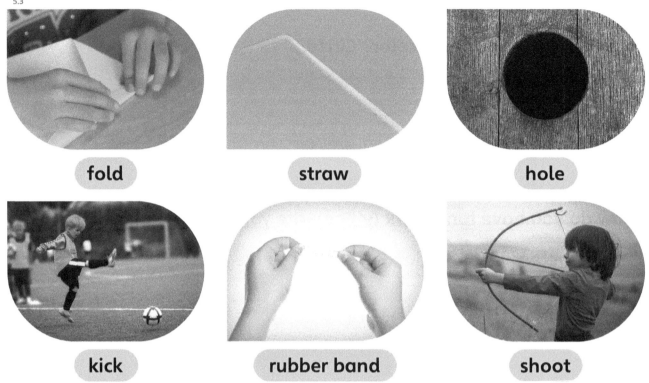

fold

straw

hole

kick

rubber band

shoot

2 Circle the actions.

f o l d s h o o t r u b b e r b a n d s t r a w k i c k h o l e

Pre-reading

3 Look at the pictures on pages 65–67. Circle the materials you can see in the pictures.

4 🎧 Listen and read.
5.4

Make Your Own Toys

By Jeremy Edgar

It is raining outside. You want to play inside. Why not make a new toy?

Making toys is fun!

Use your imagination. Look around. What can you find? **Fold** a piece of paper to make an airplane. Or you can use paper towel rolls to make a robot!

Here are some ideas!

Make a Soccer Game

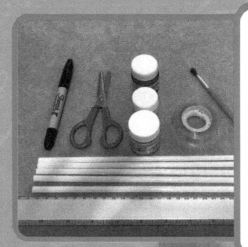

You need:
construction paper
markers or paint
scissors
a ruler
3 straws
tape
a ping-pong ball

First, make a soccer player.

1 Draw your player on construction paper.
2 Draw two circles for the legs.
3 Color or paint your player.
4 Cut out your player.
5 Cut out the circles to make **holes** for the legs.

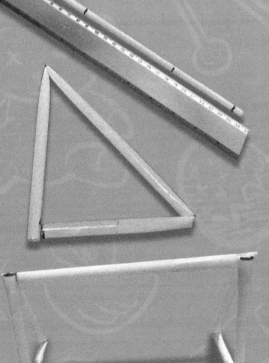

Then, make a goal.

1 Place the ruler next to a straw.
2 Measure 8cm. Draw a line with the marker
3 Measure 18cm. Draw a line with the marker.
4 Measure 25cm. Draw a line with the marker
5 Fold the straw to make a goal post.
6 Make another goal post.
7 Cut another straw in half for the bar at the top of the goal.
8 Tape the bar to the goal posts.

Now, play soccer with your friends. Put your fingers through the holes in your player. Your fingers are the player's legs! Use them to **kick** the ping-pong ball!

Make a Marshmallow Shooter

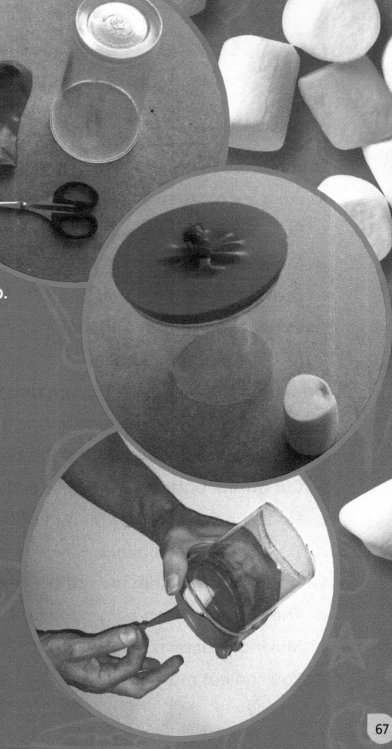

You need:
a plastic cup
a balloon
a rubber band
scissors
marshmallows

Instructions:

1 Cut off the bottom of the plastic cup.
2 Tie a knot in the balloon.
3 Cut off the other end of the balloon.
4 Place the balloon over the top of the cup.
5 Put the rubber band around the balloon.

Now you are ready to play. Put a marshmallow in the cup. Pull the knot of the balloon. Then, let go!

Can you shoot the marshmallows into a bowl? Try shooting marshmallows into your friend's mouth!

Key Words

1 **Match the Key Words to the photos.**

fold   shoot   hole   straw

Comprehension

2 **Number the instructions in order.**

Make a Soccer Game

a Put your fingers through the holes. ☐

b Make a goal. ☐

c Draw your player. ☐

d Cut out your player and make holes for the legs. ☐

e Kick the ping-pong ball. ☐

3 **Underline the first step in green and the last step in blue.**

Make a Marshmallow Shooter

a Put the rubber band around the balloon.

b Cut off the bottom of a plastic cup.

c Place the balloon over the top of the cup.

d Tie a knot in the balloon.

4 **Underline the main idea of the text.**

a The soccer ball is a ping-pong ball.

b Making your own toys is fun.

c You can eat marshmallows.

Digging Deeper

5 Which object do you need to make both toys?

_____

6 Which toy is the most difficult to make?

_____

7 Which toy is the most fun to play with?

_____

Personalization

8 Choose colors for your soccer team. Color.

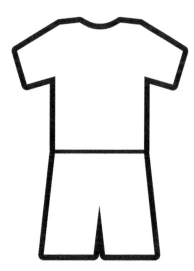

9 What do you shoot at with your Marshmallow Shooter? Draw.

6 How can we help?

Key Words

1 🎧 **Preview the Key Words.**
6.1

drop   goalie   butter

salt   cake   careful

2 Which three Key Words are things you can eat? Write the words.

_____   _____   _____

Pre-reading

3 Look at the title and pictures on pages 71–73. What do you think the name "Butterfingers" means? Circle.

a a good soccer player

b a person with butter on their fingers

c a person who drops things

4 🎧 **Listen and read.**
6.2

Oh, Butterfingers!

By Paul Drury

Illustrated by Diana Santos

Sam is named Sam. But nobody calls him Sam. Everybody calls him "Butterfingers." He drops everything.

Sam is a happy boy. He likes drawing pictures. He likes helping at home. And he loves playing soccer. He really wants to be a goalie. But he isn't very good at soccer. Sam always drops the ball. But he tries and tries. Everyone likes Sam because he tries so hard!

"Oh, Butterfingers!" say his friends. "Nice try!"

Sam doesn't understand. He looks at his fingers.

"My fingers aren't made of butter. I don't understand. Why do I drop everything?"

Sam has lots of chores. He takes out the trash. But he often drops the trash. Then, he cleans it up.

"Oh, Butterfingers!" says Dad. "Nice try!"

He sets the table. He drops the salt. Then, he sweeps the floor.

"Oh, Butterfingers," says Mom. "Nice try!"

Sam looks at his fingers. "But my fingers aren't made of butter. I don't understand. Why do I drop everything?"

Today is Sam's birthday. He's very happy. All his family and friends are at the party. There is a red and white cake. It looks yummy!

Sam's dad picks up the cake. He's very careful.
Suddenly, everything goes wrong.
The cat goes "MEOW" and runs into Sam's dad.

"Oh, no, the cake!"

The cake flies in the air.
Everybody looks at the cake. But not Sam.
He jumps and ... he catches
the cake!

All his friends say: "Wow! Nice catch, Sam! You're not a butterfingers after all!"

Sam thinks for a moment.
He says, "It's OK, you can still call me Butterfingers. I like it!"

"Now, can we have some cake, please?"

Key Words

1 **Complete the sentences with the Key Words.**

cake	careful	butter	drop	salt	goalie

a I like _____ on my pancakes.

b My sister is the _____ on her soccer team.

c This tomato soup needs more _____.

d Be _____ when you ride your bike.

e Do you prefer cookies or a piece of _____?

f Don't _____ the eggs!

Comprehension

2 **Circle *Yes* or *No*.**

a Sam is a great goalie.   Yes   No

b Sam helps his mom.   Yes   No

c Sam likes the name "Butterfingers."   Yes   No

d Sam is sad at his birthday party.   Yes   No

e Sam drops the cake.   Yes   No

f Sam tries hard.   Yes   No

3 **Mark (✔) what Sam drops.**

4 **Look at Activity 3 on page 70. Why is Sam's nickname "Butterfingers"?**

a because he catches the cake

b because he drops things

c because he's a good helper

Digging Deeper

5 📥 **Match the details to the main idea.**

draw pictures

take out the trash

sweep the floor

Chores at Home

set the table

play soccer

6 **Why do people like Sam? Underline the correct option.**

a Sam is a good goalie.

b He tries and tries.

c He drops things.

d He's very funny.

Personalization

7 **Mark (✔) the scene from the story you think is the funniest.**

8 **Imagine your nickname is "Butterfingers." Draw yourself dropping something.**

6 How can we help?

Key Words

1 🎧 **Preview the Key Words.**
6.3

feed

drink (v)

water (v)

dinner

early

late

2 **Which three Key Words are actions? Write the words.**

_____   _____   _____

Pre-reading

3 **Look at the pictures on pages 77–79. Circle what is *not* included on mom's list.**

4 🎧 **Listen and read.**
6.4

Mom's List

Mom is gone this week. She's in Chicago. She's working there. Here's her list of chores for us kids to do.

• Water the plants.

← Look! This is a happy plant.

And this is a sad plant. →

Please water the plants on Monday, Wednesday, and Friday.
Then, our plants will be happy and healthy!
Don't forget to water the lemon tree!

• Feed the dog and cat.
Rex and Daisy need to eat!
Please feed Rex and Daisy in the morning and at night.

Make sure they have water to drink!

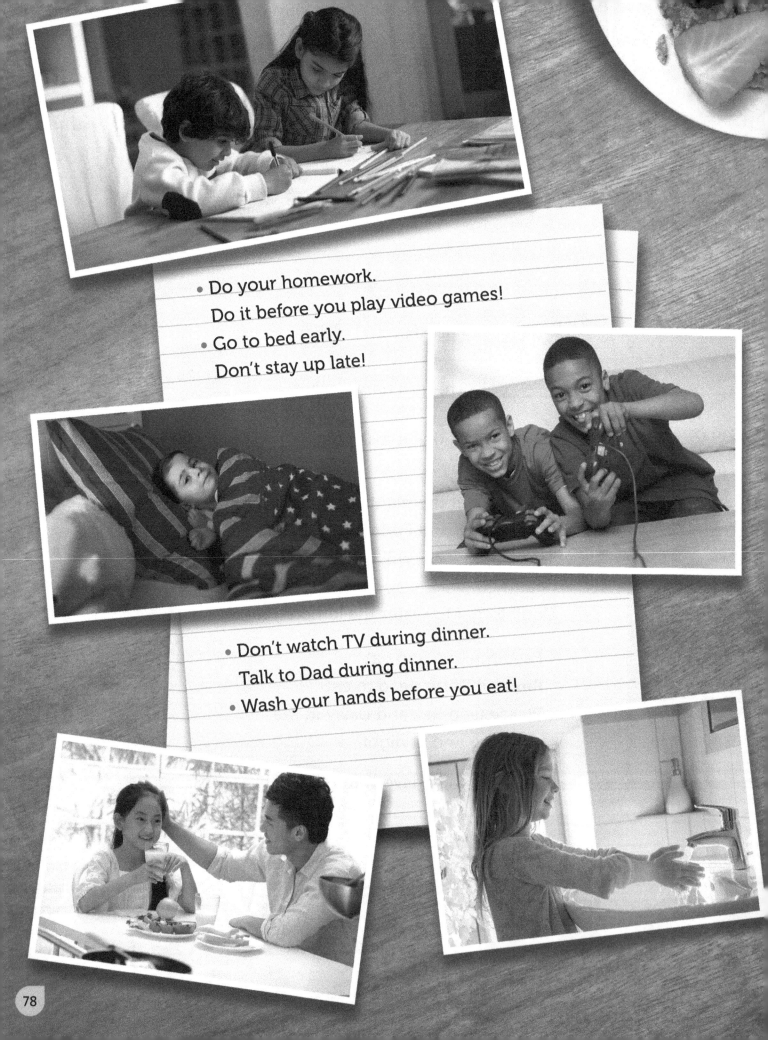

- Do your homework.
  Do it before you play video games!
- Go to bed early.
  Don't stay up late!

- Don't watch TV during dinner.
  Talk to Dad during dinner.
- Wash your hands before you eat!

- Help Dad.

- Take out the trash. Don't forget to recycle.

- Clean your rooms when they are messy.

- Put your dirty clothes in the hamper.

- Set the table for dinner.

- Call me.
Let's talk on Thursday evening.
I want to see your happy faces!

Love,
Mom

Key Words

1 **Complete the sentences with the Key Words.**

> late   feed   early   water   dinner   drink

a Please _____ your goldfish. It's hungry.

b Hurry! It's _____.The school bus is here!

c I do my homework after _____.

d You get up at 5 o'clock every morning? That's _____!

e Do you _____ milk at dinner?

f They always _____ the garden at night.

Comprehension

2 **Number the pictures.**

1 Clean your room.

2 Do your homework.

3 Wash your hands.

4 Talk to Dad during dinner.

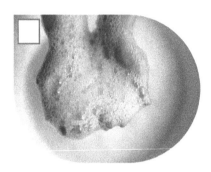

3 **Complete the sentences with the words in the box.**

> before   table   bed   Wednesday

a Please water the plants on Monday, _____, and Friday.

b Do your homework _____ you play video games!

c Go to _____ early.

d Set the _____ for dinner every day.

Digging Deeper

4 📖 **Underline the two main ideas from page 77.**

a This is a happy plant.

b Don't forget to water the lemon tree.

c Water the plants.

d Feed the dog and cat.

5 **Mom says "Talk to Dad at dinner." Circle why.**

a To spend time with Dad.

b To do homework with him.

c To teach Dad math.

Personalization

6 **Mark (✔) the things on the list that you do at home.**

take out trash

clean room

set table

water plants

feed pets

do homework

7 **Imagine another chore. Draw yourself doing the chore at home.**

7 Why do we need plants and animals?

Key Words

1 🎧 **Preview the Key Words.**
7.1

farm

plant (v)

fall

harvest

giant

delicious

2 **Write Key Words with the same meaning as the words in bold.**

a It's a **very big** monster!   _____

b That's a **yummy** cake.   _____

c They **pick** carrots on the farm.   _____

Pre-reading

3 **Look at the pictures on pages 83–85. What do you think the problem in the story is? Circle.**

a The children and animals can't pull out the plant.

b The goat is too big.

c The plant is too small.

4 🎧 **Listen and read.**
7.2

The Giant Turnip

Russian Folktale • Adapted by Jeremy Edgar
Illustrated by Gabriela Granados

Peter lives on a farm. One day, his grandfather visits.
"I have a gift for you," Peter's grandfather tells him.
He gives Peter a seed.
"This is a turnip seed," his grandfather says.
"Plant it now. Then, wait until fall."
Peter plants the seed in the soil.

Now it is fall. Peter wakes up.
The morning air is cold.

"It's time to harvest my turnip,"
Peter thinks.

Peter goes out to see the turnip.
He can't believe his eyes.
The turnip is very big. Peter pulls
at the turnip. He pulls very hard.

Peter calls his sister, Karen.
Peter pulls the turnip. Karen pulls
Peter. They pull and pull, but they
can't pull out the turnip.

Karen calls the goat. The goat pulls Karen. Karen pulls Peter. Peter pulls
the turnip. They pull and pull, but they can't pull out the turnip.

The goat calls the dog. The dog pulls the goat. The goat pulls Karen. Karen pulls Peter. Peter pulls the turnip. They pull and pull, but they can't pull out the turnip.

The dog calls the chick. The chick pulls the dog. The dog pulls the goat. The goat pulls Karen. Karen pulls Peter. Peter pulls the turnip. They pull and pull, but they can't pull out the turnip.

The chick calls the mouse. The mouse pulls the chick. The chick pulls the dog. The dog pulls the goat. The goat pulls Karen. Karen pulls Peter, Peter pulls the turnip. They pull and pull and pull. Finally, out comes the giant turnip!

"Nice job, everyone!" Peter says. "Now, let's all eat this delicious turnip!"

Key Words

1 **Circle the correct Key Word.**

a It is summer / fall. It is time to harvest the turnip.

b Peter plants / harvests the seed in the soil.

c Peter lives on a playground / farm.

2 **Complete the sentences with Key Words.**

a Farmers _____ fruit in the fall.

b Leaves change color in _____.

c There are chicks and goats on a _____.

Comprehension

3 **Write *T* (true) or *F* (false).**

a Peter's grandfather gives him a seed. _____

b Peter harvests the turnip in spring. _____

c The animals don't help Peter. _____

4 **Who pulls out the giant turnip? Label the animals and people from the story.**

Peter _____   _____   _____

_____   _____   _____

5 **Number the animals and people in Activity 4 in order.**

Digging Deeper

6 **What does this tale teach us? Circle.**

    a There are a lot of animals on a farm.

    b Turnips are delicious.

    c Working as a team is important.

7 **Visualize a different ending and draw it.**

Personalization

8 **What's your favorite animal from the story?**

My favorite animal is the _____.

9 **Choose another animal to help Peter. Draw it and write its name.**

_____

7 Why do we need plants and animals?

Key Words

1 **Preview the Key Words.**
7.3

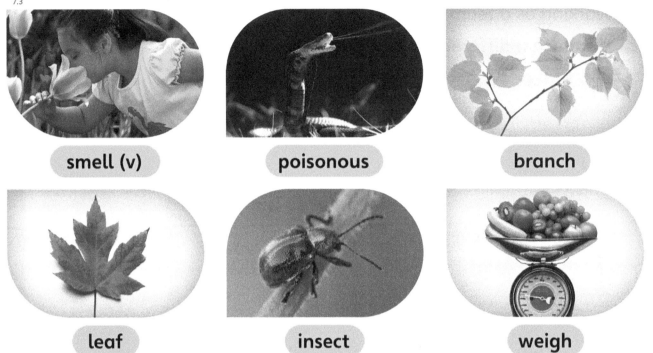

smell (v)   poisonous   branch

leaf   insect   weigh

2 **Circle the correct Key Word.**

a The flowers weigh / smell good.

b That tree has very large branches / insects. I can climb on them!

c Some insects in the Amazon are smell / poisonous.

d The branches / leaves change colors in the fall.

Pre-reading

3 **Look at the subtitles and pictures on pages 89–91. Answer the questions.**

a How many plants does the article describe? _____

b Which plant looks like it has eyes? _____

c Which plant looks like a ball? _____

d Do any of these plants look familiar? _____

4 **Listen and read.**
7.4

AMAZING PLANTS

By Lily Pane

What are plants? They are living organisms.

Plants are

big

or

small.

Some plants smell good.

Some plants smell terrible.

Do you like plants? Look at these amazing plants.

Baneberry Plant

These are red and white baneberries. The fruits of this plant are poisonous. White baneberries are called "doll's eyes." Can you guess why?

Baseball Plant

This plant is from South Africa. It is similar to a baseball! Does it have branches? No. Can you eat this plant? No, it's poisonous.

Shy Plant

This plant is from Central and South America. When you touch it, its leaves close!

Its flowers are purple or pink.

Venus Flytrap

The Venus flytrap is a carnivorous plant. "Carnivorous" means that it eats meat. This plant eats small insects! It takes the plant 5 to 12 days to digest them.

Look at the leaves. They have tiny hairs. Can you see them?

You can have a Venus flytrap at home!

Pitcher Plant

This plant is also carnivorous. It smells nice. It eats animals like lizards, mice, spiders, and worms!

Corpse Flower

This flower is very big.
It is also very heavy.
It weighs around 90 kilos!

What's that horrible smell?
It is the corpse flower!

Dragon's Blood Tree

What is this tree similar to?
That's right! An umbrella!
It can live for 650 years.
It is 10 to 12 meters tall.
This tree produces a red
substance. It looks similar
to blood!

Baobab Tree

There are baobabs in Africa,
Madagascar, and Australia.
This tree is 5 to 20 meters tall.
It can live for 2,500 years!
The baobab is the tree of life.
Its leaves and fruit are food for
people and animals. You can make
medicine from its fruit! It provides
water to animals who eat its bark.

Plants are amazing! Which one is your favorite?

Key Words

1 **Complete the sentences with the correct Key Words.**

a The corpse flower s_____ horrible.

b The corpse flower is also very big. It w_____ almost 100 kilos!

c An i_____ can be inside a Venus flytrap for many days.

d When you touch the l_____ of a shy plant, it closes.

e You can't eat baneberries. They are p_____.

f The baseball plant doesn't have any b_____.

Comprehension

2 **Match the plants to the objects they are similar to.**

| 1 Dragon's Blood Tree | 2 Baseball Plant |

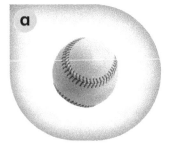 a

 b

 c

 d

3 **Match the plants to the captions.**

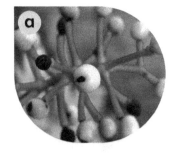 a

 b

 c

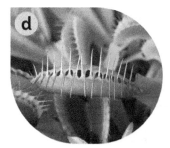 d

1 This tree is similar to an umbrella. _____

2 The leaves of this plant have hairs. _____

3 The fruits are similar to a doll's eyes. _____

4 This flower is very big. _____

Digging Deeper

4 **Circle the correct option.**

1 Which carnivorous plant can eat bigger animals?

    a the pitcher plant

    b the Venus flytrap

2 The baobab tree is called the "tree of life." Why?

    a It drinks lots of water.

    b People and animals eat its fruit.

3 Why is the dragon's blood tree called that?

    a It produces a red substance that looks like blood.

    b It has red flowers. They look like dragons.

Personalization

5 **Choose your three favorite plants from the text and draw them.**

2   1   3

6 **Imagine an amazing new plant and draw it. Write its name.**

Name: _____

8 What is imagination?

Key Words

1 🎧 **Preview the Key Words.**
8.1

kiss (v)

sleepy

carpet

secret

boat

huge

2 **Which Key Word is an action? Write the word.**

_____

3 **Which Key Words can describe people or things? Write the words.**

_____   _____

Pre-reading

4 **Look at pages 95–99. Then, circle the characters from the story.**

5 🎧 **Listen and read.**
8.2

Imagine That!

By Sarah Steinberg

Illustrated by Isabel Gómez

It's bedtime. Win and his mom read
a story. Then, Win gets into bed.
Mom kisses him on the head.

"I'm not tired," Win says.

"That's OK," Mom says.
You can just relax.
Use your imagination."

"What's that?" says Win.

"Imagination is what you use
to make up a story.
You can imagine anything
you want."

Win thinks about this.
It's a good idea.
He wants to try it.
But not now.
Now he is sleepy.

It's morning. Win wakes up. He goes downstairs.
His dad is in the kitchen. He is frying eggs.

"Good morning, Win. How did you sleep?" asks his dad.

"Good," says Win. Then, he uses his imagination.

"But...," says Win, "My teddy bear woke me up early.
He was hungry."

"I see," his dad says. "Let's feed him.
And what about you? Are you hungry?"

Dad puts the eggs on a plate.

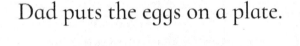
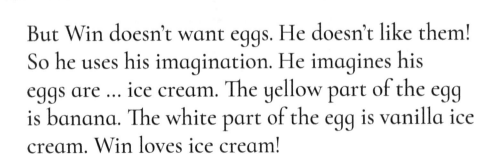

But Win doesn't want eggs. He doesn't like them!
So he uses his imagination. He imagines his
eggs are ... ice cream. The yellow part of the egg
is banana. The white part of the egg is vanilla ice
cream. Win loves ice cream!

Win eats up his ice cream. Yum!

After breakfast, Win gets dressed for school.

"All right everybody," says his mom. "Get your things. We don't want to be late!"

Win's big brother is putting on his shoes. Win tries to tie his shoelaces quickly, but he can't. It's hard!

"Don't be a slowpoke," says Win's big brother.

"Let's go, Win," says Dad.

Win imagines that he can go very fast. Faster than an airplane! Zoom! Shoes on, zoom! Jacket on, zoom! Backpack, zoom! Ready!

At school, Win uses his imagination all day. He imagines his paintbrush is a magic wand. He imagines the carpet is a jungle. He imagines all his friends speak a secret language.

At recess, Win climbs on the play structure.
He climbs to the top. He imagines he is the captain of a boat.
He drives the boat on top of big waves. Now he can see a whale.
A huge gray whale!

At home, Win wants to play with his big brother. His big brother does not want to play with him.

"You're too little!" his big brother says. He closes his bedroom door. Win is sad.

So Win uses his imagination. He imagines he is not little. He is bigger than his brother. In fact, he is the biggest kid in the whole world. He is so big he can play basketball with the moon. That's how big he is!

It is time for bed. Win and his mom read a book. Then, she gives him a kiss.

"Are you sleepy?" his mom asks.

"No," says Win. "But that's OK. I'm going to imagine I am!"

Key Words

1 **Complete with Key Words.**

Comprehension

2 **Who says what? Write the name of the character.**

Win	Mom	Dad	Brother

a "Use your imagination." _____

b "Are you hungry?" _____

c "You're too little!" _____

d "Are you sleepy?" _____

e "I'm not tired." _____

3 **What does Win imagine? Match.**

1 carpet   a magic wand

2 eggs   b jungle

3 paintbrush   c basketball

4 play structure   d boat

5 moon   e ice cream

Digging Deeper

4 📧 **Mark (✔) the correct summary of *Imagine That!***

Summary I ☐
Win learns how to use his imagination in his everyday life.

Summary 2 ☐
Win imagines his eggs are ice cream.

5 **Use your imagination. Draw.**

Win is on the moon.

The moon is blue.

Win is eating

vanilla ice cream.

He is happy.

Personalization

6 **Answer the questions.**

a Do you like ice cream? _____

b Can you tie your shoelaces? _____

7 **What's your favorite part of the story? Draw a picture.**

8 What is imagination?

Key Words

1 🎧 **Preview the Key Words**
8.3

amazing   creature   strange

wave   stripes   spots

2 **Complete the sentences with the correct Key Words.**

a A tiger has _____.

b A leopard has _____.

c They are both _____ creatures!

Pre-reading

3 **Look at the pictures on pages 103–105. Write T (true) or F (false).**

a The text is about an art project.   _____

b The creatures are real.   _____

c You need scissors.   _____

d You need balloons.   _____

4 🎧 **Listen and read.**
8.4

A Sea Creature of Your Imagination

By Jeremy Edgar

Imagine you are in the ocean.
You can see lots of amazing sea creatures!
There is a big purple fish next to you.
Now you see an octopus on a rock.
It waves at you. You wave back.
Then, you see another sea creature.
It's very strange. Be careful!

Look! The creature is friendly!
It swims closer to you.
What is this sea creature like?
Is it big or small?
What color is it?
Does it have stripes?
Does it have spots?
Does it have a tail?
Does it have legs?
Does it have fins?
Does it have claws?
Close your eyes now and use
your imagination.

You need:

white paper

a pencil

a black marker

a paintbrush

scissors

glue

paints

Make a painting of your imaginary sea creature.

1. With a pencil, draw a sea creature.

2. Draw patterns and shapes on your creature.

3. With a black marker, trace over the pencil.

4. Paint your sea creature.

5. Let your painting dry.

6. With scissors, cut out your sea creature.

Make a classroom sea poster with your classmates.

1. Paint the poster board blue.

2. Let the paint dry.

3. Paint rocks and plants at the bottom.

4. Glue your sea creature onto the poster.

Anna

5. Write your name on a piece of paper. Then, cut it out.

6. Glue your name label next to your sea creature.

Now look at all the amazing sea creatures. What a great imagination!

Key Words

1 Look and circle *T* (true) or *F* (false).

a This sea creature is imaginary. T F
b It has spots. T F
c It has stripes. T F
d It is waving. T F
e It is strange. T F
f It is amazing. T F

This is a baby cuttlefish.

Comprehension

2 Match.

draw

glue

paint

write

cut

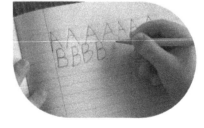

3 Number the steps in order.

_____ Draw patterns and shapes on your creature.

_____ Draw a sea creature.

_____ Cut out your sea creature.

_____ Paint your sea creature.

Digging Deeper

4 Label the pictures.

first   next   last

a _____

b _____

c _____

Personalization

5 Imagine a sea creature and draw it. Then, answer the questions.

a What color is your sea creature?

_____

b Is it big or small?

_____

c Does it have spots or stripes?

_____

d What does it eat?

_____

e What is your sea creature's name?

_____

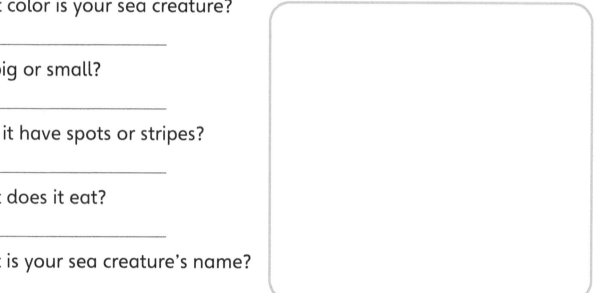

6 Color a face for each question.

a Do you like sea creatures?

b Do you like the art project?

c Do you clean up after art projects?

9 Why do we need clothes?

Key Words

1  **Preview the Key Words.**
9.1

hat   head   shirt

back   hang   rack

2 **Circle the correct Key Word.**

a Please hang your coat on the rack / head.

b Joe is wearing a white rack / shirt, brown pants, and red shoes.

c I love your picture. Let's hang / back it on the wall.

d There is a butterfly on the back / head of my shirt.

Pre-reading

3 **Look at the illustrations on pages 109–111 and write four kinds of clothes you see.**

a _____   c _____

b _____   d _____

4 **Listen and read.**
9.2

My Hat Is Dancing on My Head

By Kenn Nesbitt • Illustrated by Emmanuel Urueta

My hat is dancing
on my head.
It is not sleeping
in a bed.
My hat is blue,
not green or red.
It has a name.
I call it "Fred."

My shirt is dancing
on my back.
It is not hanging
on a rack.
My shirt is blue,
not brown or black.
It has a name.
I call it "Jack."

My pants are dancing
with my shoe.
Like all my clothes,
they too are blue.
My pants are "Lance."
My shoe is "Lou."
Does all of this
sound true to you?

Key Words

1 **Circle the word that doesn't belong.**

a   back   head   red   hand

b   dance   sleep   hat   hang

c   rack   shirt   pants   shoes

Comprehension

2 **Read the poem again and answer.**

The clothes are dancing. What aren't they doing? Circle.

a   The hat isn't **hanging on a rack** / **sleeping in a bed.**

b   The shirt isn't **hanging on a rack** / **sleeping in a bed.**

3 **Label the clothes. Then, match them to their names.**

a _____

b _____

c _____

d _____

Jack

Lou

Fred

Lance

Digging Deeper

4 📖 **Write MI (main idea) and D (details) for each set of sentences.**

1 a The man's clothes have names.   _____

   b The hat's name is "Fred."   _____

   c The shoe's name is "Lou."   _____

2 a The man's pants dance with his shoe.   _____

   b The man's clothes dance.   _____

   c The man's hat dances on his head.   _____

5 **Complete the sentences with the correct options.**

   a The word "shoe" rhymes with _____.

   Fred   Lou

   b The word "black" rhymes with _____.

   Jack   Lance

   c The word "red" rhymes with _____.

   Lance   Fred

   d The word "pants" rhymes with _____.

   Lou   Lance

Personalization

6 **Match the colors to the correct names to create rhyming pairs.**

   blue   green   red   black

   Zack   Ted   Dean   Sue

7 **Complete the poem with new words. Remember lines 2 and 4 rhyme.**

   1 My hat is _(color)_____,

   2 not white or _(color)_____.

   3 It has a name.

   4 I call it "_____."

9 Why do we need clothes?

Key Words

1 **Preview the Key Words.**
9.3

sandals   protect   step on

leather   strong   fur

2 **Complete the sentences with the Key Words.**

> protect   step on   strong   leather

a He's wearing a _____ jacket.

b She's a _____ girl!

c Be careful! Don't _____ that toy!

d The umbrellas _____ the boys from the rain.

Pre-reading

3 **Read the first two lines of the text on page 115 and answer the question.**

What kind of shoes are you wearing?

I'm wearing _____.

4 **Listen and read.**
9.4

Happy Feet Around the World

By Lily Pane

Are you wearing shoes today?
Are they sandals, boots, or tennis shoes?
Or are they dress shoes for school?

Why do we wear shoes? Shoes protect
our feet. They protect them from
cold, hot, snowy, and rainy weather.
They also protect our feet from
insects and hard objects.

I'm not wearing shoes today.
Ouch! I stepped on something!
It hurts! What is it? Is it a rock?

Put on your
shoes, Mitch!

What shoes do you like to wear? Why?
There are many types of shoes around the world.

These shoes are from Japan. They are called *geta*. They are made of wood. Girls wear geta with kimonos. Kimonos are traditional Japanese dresses.

Geta

Kimono

Now let's go to Mexico. These are *huaraches*. They are leather sandals. They are strong! The Rarámuri people can run very far in *huaraches*. Amazing!

Huaraches

Jutti

Do you know what *jutti* are? They are leather shoes from India. They have beautiful designs. People wear them to weddings and festivals.

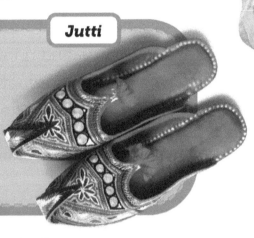

Brrr ... The Sámi people live in cold places. They wear boots for very cold weather.

These boots are made of reindeer fur. Look at the toes! Why are they like that? So it is easy to ski with them!

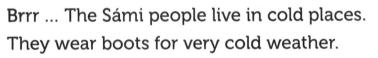

Reindeer fur boots

116

Cowboy boots are made of leather. It's easy to ride a horse with cowboy boots.

Cowboy boots

There are other unique shoes around the world, but people do not wear them now. Look at these shoes from the past!

These are Roman sandals.

These shoes protected feet from mud and snow. They were used in Sweden, Norway, and Russia.

These are clogs from Holland. They are made of wood.

Some of the shoes we wear today are similar to shoes from the past. Look! Which shoes are these similar to?

Key Words

1 **Complete the sentences with the correct Key Words.**

a Shoes _____ our feet.

b *Huaraches* are leather _____.

c Sámi people wear boots made of reindeer _____.

d Leather is a very _____ material.

Comprehension

2 **Rewrite the sentences so that they are true. Change the underlined word.**

a Japanese girls wear *geta* with <u>pants</u>.

_____

b <u>*Huaraches*</u> are from India.

_____

c The Sámi people wear boots for <u>rainy</u> weather.

_____

d The Rarámuri people can run very far in <u>boots</u>.

_____

3 **Complete the table.**

What are the shoes made of?

| geta | huaraches | jutti | Sámi boots | cowboy boots | clogs |

Leather	Wood	Fur

Digging Deeper

4 🔊 **Circle the best summary of the text.**

   a Cowboys wear boots to ride horses.

   b Sámi boots are for cold weather.

   c Shoes protect our feet.

   d Clogs are made of wood.

5 **What can shoes protect your feet from? Circle the correct options.**

hot sand   candy   butterflies   ice

rain   socks   ants   spiders

Personalization

6 **Which shoes from the text are your favorite?**

My favorite shoes are _____.

7 **Design a pair of unique shoes.**

Acknowledgments

The authors and publishers acknowledge the following sources of copyright material and are grateful for the permissions granted. While every effort has been made, it has not always been possible to identify the sources of all the material used or to trace all copyright holders. If any omissions are brought to our notice, we will be happy to include the appropriate acknowledgments on reprinting and in the next update to the digital edition, as applicable.

Key: U = Unit.

Photographs

All the photos are sourced from Getty Images.

U1: Rakdee/DigitalVision Vectors; FingerMedium/DigitalVision Vectors; Enis Aksoy/DigitalVision Vectors; Peathegee Inc; Sally Anscombe/DigitalVision; tatyana_tomsickova/iStock/Getty Images Plus; Burcu Atalay Tankut/Moment; Mrs_2015/RooM; J and J Productions/DigitalVision; shapecharge/E+; Petar Chernaev/E+; Eric Audras/ONOKY; Steven Beijer/EyeEm; filadendron/E+; hdagli/E+; Anna Kurzaeva/Moment; ONOKY - Eric Audras/Brand X Pictures; Jose Luis Pelaez Inc/DigitalVision; Ariel Skelley/DigitalVision; Morsa Images/DigitalVision; Imgorthand/E+; Eskay Lim/EyeEM; **U2:** Jeffrey Penalosa/EyeEm; JGI; Donald Iain Smith/Moment; R.Tsubin/Moment; Alistair Berg/DigitalVision; Kinzie Riehm/Image Source; rangepuppies/DigitalVision Vectors; bubaone/DigitalVision Vectors; 4x6/DigitalVision Vectors; appleuzr/DigitalVision Vectors; Jose Luis Pelaez Inc/DigitalVision; Westend61; fatihhoca/E+; RUNSTUDIO/Moment; Capelle.r/Moment; JGI/Jamie Grill; Eskay Lim/EyeEm; Noel Yeow/500px; fcafotodigital/E+; deepblue4you/E+; EyeEm; paci77/E+; jabiru/iStock/Getty Images Plus; hudiemm/E+; RedHelga/E+; natrot/iStock/Getty Images Plus; Sarah Saratonina/EyeEm; george tsartsianidis/iStock/Getty Images Plus; sarahdoow/iStock/Getty Images Plus; iuliia_n/iStock/Getty Images Plus; Massimiliano Clari/EyeEm; Nattawut Lakjit/EyeEm; FuatKose/E+; Science Photo Library; ThitareeSarmkasat/iStock/Getty Images Plus; Blend Images - JGI/Jamie Grill; Philippe Desnerck/Photolibrary; dontree_m/iStock/Getty Images Plus; Vasuta Thitayarak/EyeEm; Peter Langer/Design Pics; **U3:** Wan Fahmy Redzuan Wan Muhammad/EyeEm; Eskay Lim/EyeEm; firina/iStock/Getty Images Plus; Conrado Tramontini/Moment; Anass Bachar/EyeEm; Christina Reichl Photography/Moment; PATSTOCK/Moment; Puneet Vikram Singh, Nature and Concept photographer/Moment; WIN-Initiative/Neleman/Stone; Maisie Paterson; Imgorthand/E+; ViewStock; Blend Images - JGI/Jamie Grill; Mayur Kakade/Moment; Nicholas Reuss/500px; Ivan Ferdian/EyeEm; Mohamad Ridzuan Abdul Rashid/EyeEm; Matteo Tessarotto/EyeEm; Tjasa Smrekar/EyeEm; retales botijero/Moment; Feri Bellamy/EyeEm; Rian Krenzer/500px; Chris Winsor/Moment; Photogore/Moment Open; Cyndi Monaghan/Moment; Michelle Pinto/EyeEm; EyeEm; Sarah Saratonina/EyeEm; PeopleImages/E+; Mint Images/Paul Edmondson/Mint Images RF; Debby Lewis-Harrison/Cultura; Busybee-CR/Moment; klosfoto/E+; **U4:** Sol Estravis/EyeEm; Imgorthand/E+; ZenShui/Michele Constantini/PhotoAlto Agency RF Collections; Anna Pekunova/Moment; Lauren Bates/Moment; Westend61; EyeEm; Constantine Johnny/Moment; Jose Luis Pelaez Inc/DigitalVision; Christina Reichl Photography/Moment; Thanit Weerawan/Moment; Ivan Hunter/Photodisc; simonlong/Moment; IP Galanternik D.U./E+; **U5:** Theerasak Tammachuen/EyeEm; AYImages/E+; Mezei Zsanett/EyeEm; plusphoto; Johner Images; Teen00000/iStock/Getty Images Plus; Jasmin Merdan/Moment; rustemgurler/E+; EyeEm; YouraPechkin/iStock/Getty Images Plus; enjoynz/DigitalVision Vectors; South_agency/E+; Westend61; Radomir Tarasov/EyeEm; Getty Images/iStockphoto; shironosov/iStock/Getty Images Plus; paylessimages/iStock/Getty Images Plus; bubaone/DigitalVision Vectors; **U6:** Matejay/E+;

Ashli Hilley/EyeEm; Caspar Benson; EyeEm; Woraphon Nusen/EyeEm; Aniko Hobel/Moment; alex_ugalek/iStock/Getty Images Plus; sam thomas/iStock/Getty Images Plus; Tetra Images - Mike Kemp/Brand X Pictures; jhorrocks/E+; mikroman6/Moment; Image Source; sunara/E+; mashabuba/E+; Flavio Coelho/Moment; PeopleImages/E+; Andersen Ross Photography Inc/DigitalVision; Catherine Delahaye/DigitalVision; View Stock; mrs/Moment; Juanmonino/E+; Kentaroo Tryman/Maskot; Jose Luis Pelaez Inc/DigitalVision; fatihhoca/iStock/Getty Images Plus; Westend61; Deanna Hammond/FOAP/foap; MakiEni's photo/Moment; Ryan McVay/Photodisc; 10'000 Hours/DigitalVision; Ned Frisk; Comstock Images/Stockbyte; Maskot; Halfpoint Images/Moment; Johner Images; **U7:** bigjom/iStock/Getty Images Plus; dragance137/iStock/Getty Images Plus; urfinguss/iStock/Getty Images Plus; jamielawton/DigitalVision Vectors; bkkm/iStock/Getty Images Plus; passion4nature/iStock/Getty Images Plus; Egmont Strigl; REDA&CO/Universal Images Group; AlonzoDesign/DigitalVision Vectors; A-Digit/DigitalVision Vectors; Leontura/DigitalVision Vectors; hakule/DigitalVision Vectors; DigitalVision; Cornelia Doerr/Photographer's Choice RF; Roc Canals/Moment; EyeEm; Jonathan Kitchen/DigitalVision; Jake Jung/Moment; Unggul Wicaksono/Moment; sarra22/iStock/Getty Images Plus; tkhatsko/iStock/Getty Images Plus; juhajarvinen/iStock/Getty Images Plus; shihina/iStock/Getty Images Plus; JokoHarismoyo/iStock/Getty Images Plus; Ed Reschke/Photodisc; REDA&CO/Universal Images Group; Auscape/Universal Images Group; Littlekiss Photography/Moment; Thanit Weerawan/Moment; Drew Angerer/Getty Images News; Csilla Zelko/500Px Plus; Sylvain CORDIER/Gamma-Rapho; Thorsten Negro; **U8:** Jose Luis Pelaez Inc/DigitalVision; Freder/E+; Westend61; Kativ/E+; Thawisak Buttharaksa/EyeEm; Grant Ordelheide/Aurora Photos; InnaBodrova/DigitalVision Vectors; pijama61/DigitalVision Vectors; aris/iStock/Getty Images Plus; EyeEm; enter89/E+; Floortje/E+; Yevgen Romanenko/Moment; skodonnell/E+; fotograzia/Moment; Carlos Bezz/Moment; somethingway/E+; Katy McDonnell/DigitalVision; Graiki/Moment; Andre Walther/Cultura; Weekend Images Inc./E+; Tetra Images; Brasil2/E+; David Harrigan; Jasmin Merdan/Moment; **U9:** Prapan Ngaokaew/EyeEm; Ng Sok Lian/EyeEm; bonetta/E+; Yevgen Romanenko/Moment; Jacobs Stock Photography Ltd/DigitalVision; Estersinhache fotografía/Moment; no_limit_pictures/iStock/Getty Images Plus; George Mdivanian/EyeEm; Sophie Walster/iStock/Getty Images Plus; Feifei Cui-Paoluzzo/Moment; Ariel Skelley/DigitalVision; SabdiZ/iStock/Getty Images Plus; Wattanaphob Kappago/EyeEm; pearleye/E+; Nattawut Lakjit/EyeEm; clu/E+; Samart Boonyang/EyeEm; hiromi kawaguchi/Moment; sot/DigitalVision; Hola Images; photosindia; Hemant Mehta; Tiina Pokka/iStock/Getty Images Plus; THEPALMER/iStock/Getty Images Plus; Stefan Rotter/iStock/Getty Images Plus; Cultura RF; Valerii Maksimov/iStock/Getty Images Plus; 01452/Corbis.

Nonfiction authors

U1: Hermione Kitson (*A Very Special Person in My Life*); **U3:** Maggie Pane (*The Amazing World of Ants*); **U4:** Liliana Rodríguez (*Best Friends Forever*); **U6:** Paul Drury (*Mom's List*).

Illustrations

Claudia Navarro; Diana Santos; Emmanuel Urueta; Gabriela Granados; Isabel Gómez; Ismael Vázquez; Laura González; Luis Montiel; Mónica Cahue.

Cover Artwork commissioned by Aphik S.A. de C.V.

Cover Illustration by Isabel Gómez.

Page make-up

Aphik S.A. de C.V.